PNEUMONIA EDUCATION FOR HEALTHCARE PROVIDERS

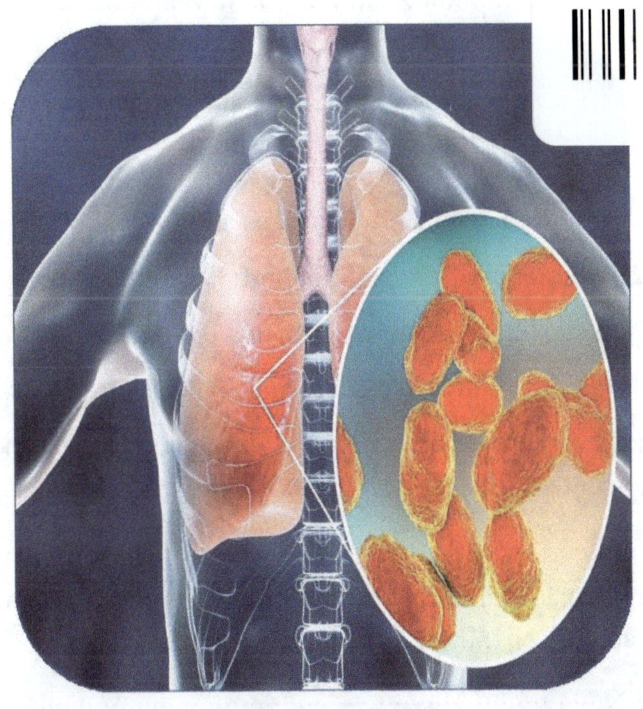

TABLE OF CONTENTS

COURSE OVERVIEW:

This course is designed to equip healthcare professionals with an in-depth understanding of pneumonia, encompassing its pathophysiology, clinical manifestations, diagnostic techniques, and treatment protocols. This course aims to enhance the knowledge and skills of respiratory therapists, doctors, and nurses in diagnosing and managing pneumonia, ensuring they are well-prepared to provide optimal patient care. Through a combination of theoretical knowledge and practical case studies, participants will explore the complexities of pneumonia in various patient populations and learn to navigate the challenges of antibiotic resistance, prevention strategies, and the integration of emerging technologies in pneumonia care.

COURSE OBJECTIVES:

By the end of this course, participants will be able to Understand the Epidemiology and Pathophysiology of Pneumonia, Identify Clinical Signs and Symptoms, Utilize Diagnostic Tools Effectively, Address Pneumonia in Special Populations Promote Prevention and Vaccination, Tackle Antibiotic Resistance, Incorporate Technology in Pneumonia Care, Understand the Role of Nutrition in Pneumonia Care, Address Psychological and Social Aspects, Navigate Legal and Ethical Considerations, Stay Updated on Future Directions. By achieving these objectives, healthcare providers will be better prepared to deliver comprehensive and effective care to patients with pneumonia, ultimately improving patient outcomes and advancing public health.

COURSE MATERIALS

To learn this course, healthcare providers/ participants must be provided with materials like a Pen, pencil, notebook, and notepad to better understand and make it easy for them to learn.

INTRODUCTION

Pneumonia, a significant cause of morbidity and mortality worldwide, is a critical area of study for healthcare providers, including respiratory therapists, doctors, and nurses. Understanding pneumonia in all its dimensions clinical presentation, physiological impact, radiological appearance, and treatment modalities is essential for effective patient care and management.

In recent years, the landscape of pneumonia has evolved, with new pathogens emerging, resistance patterns changing, and innovative treatment options becoming available. Consequently, staying updated with the latest information and best practices is crucial for healthcare providers. This book is designed to be a detailed resource that covers every aspect of pneumonia, ensuring that readers are well-prepared to handle the challenges associated with this condition.

By the end of this book, readers will have a comprehensive understanding of pneumonia, from its basic principles to advanced management strategies. This knowledge will empower healthcare providers to deliver high-quality care, improve patient outcomes, and stay at the forefront of pneumonia management.

MODULE ONE

LESSON ONE: UNDERSTANDING PNEUMONIA

Pneumonia is an infection that inflames the air sacs in one or both lungs, which can fill with fluid or pus, causing cough with phlegm or pus, fever, chills, and difficulty breathing. A variety of organisms, including bacteria, viruses, and fungi, can cause pneumonia. The severity of pneumonia can range from mild to life-threatening, with the severity being higher for infants, young children, older adults, and people with weakened immune systems.

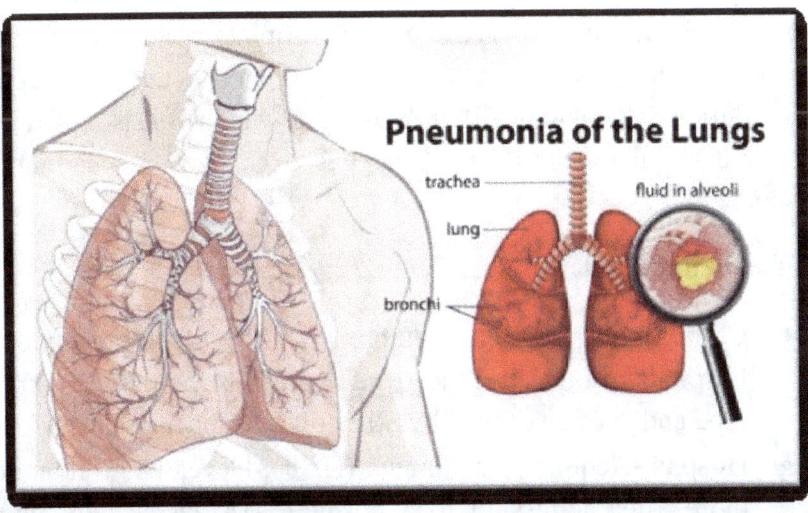

Etiology and Epidemiology

Pneumonia can be classified based on its etiology (cause) into bacterial, viral, fungal, and mycoplasma pneumonia. Bacterial pneumonia is often the most severe and is most commonly caused by Streptococcus pneumoniae. Viral pneumonia, caused by influenza viruses, respiratory syncytial virus (RSV), and others, is generally less severe but can lead to significant morbidity. Fungal pneumonia is less common and typically affects people with weakened immune systems.

Epidemiologically, pneumonia is a significant health issue worldwide. According to the World Health Organization (WHO), pneumonia accounts for 15% of all deaths of children under 5 years old, killing 740,180 children in 2019 alone. In the United States, pneumonia is a leading cause of hospitalization and death among older adults and people with chronic diseases.

Pathophysiology

The pathophysiology of pneumonia involves the invasion of the lung parenchyma by pathogens, leading to an inflammatory response. This response includes the accumulation of neutrophils, macrophages, and lymphocytes in the alveoli and interstitial spaces, causing alveolar consolidation. The alveoli fill with exudate, which consists of fluid, cells, and cellular debris, impairing gas exchange and leading to hypoxia.

Types of Pneumonia

- Community-Acquired Pneumonia (CAP): Occurs outside of hospitals or other healthcare settings. It is the most common type and is often caused by Streptococcus pneumoniae.
- Hospital-Acquired Pneumonia (HAP): Develops 48 hours or more after admission to a hospital. HAP is usually more severe than CAP due to the higher prevalence of antibiotic-resistant bacteria.
- Ventilator-Associated Pneumonia (VAP): A type of HAP that occurs in people who are on mechanical ventilation.
- Aspiration Pneumonia: Caused by inhaling food, drink, vomit, or saliva into the lungs. This type often occurs in people with swallowing difficulties or a decreased level of consciousness.

Risk Factors

Several risk factors can increase the likelihood of developing pneumonia:

- Age: Very young children and older adults are at higher risk.
- Chronic Diseases: Conditions such as asthma, chronic obstructive pulmonary disease (COPD), heart disease, and diabetes.
- Weakened Immune System: People with weakened immune systems due to conditions like HIV/AIDS, cancer treatment, or organ transplants.
- Smoking: Damages the lungs' defense mechanisms.
- Hospitalization: Particularly if in an intensive care unit (ICU) or on a ventilator.

Signs and Symptoms

- Common signs and symptoms of pneumonia include:
- Cough, which may produce greenish, yellow, or even bloody mucus
- Fever, sweating, and shaking chills
- Shortness of breath
- Rapid, shallow breathing
- Sharp or stabbing chest pain that gets worse when you breathe deeply or cough
- Loss of appetite, low energy, and fatigue
- Nausea and vomiting, especially in small children
- Confusion, especially in older people

Diagnosis

The diagnosis of pneumonia typically involves a combination of clinical assessment and diagnostic tests. Clinical assessment includes taking a thorough medical history and performing a physical examination, where a healthcare provider listens for abnormal lung sounds with a stethoscope. **Diagnostic tests may include:**

- Chest X-ray: The most common imaging test to look for pneumonia.
- Blood tests: To confirm the infection and try to identify the causative organism.
- Pulse oximetry: To measure the oxygen level in the blood.
- Sputum test: To analyze the mucus (sputum) coughed up from the lungs.
- CT scan: Provides more detailed images if pneumonia is suspected but not clearly visible on an X-ray.
- Pleural fluid culture: If fluid is present in the pleural space, a sample can be taken to identify the causative organism.

Understanding pneumonia's etiology, epidemiology, pathophysiology, types, risk factors, and diagnostic approaches is fundamental for healthcare providers. This knowledge forms the basis for effective diagnosis, treatment, and management of pneumonia, which will be explored in greater detail in subsequent lessons. By comprehensively understanding these foundational aspects, healthcare providers can improve patient outcomes and reduce the burden of pneumonia in their practice.

DISCUSSION QUESTIONS

- How do the different types of pneumonia (bacterial, viral, and fungal) affect treatment strategies for healthcare providers?
- What are the key factors that contribute to the development of pneumonia in vulnerable populations, and how can healthcare providers mitigate these risks?

LESSON TWO CLINICAL AND PHYSIOLOGICAL SIGNS OF PNEUMONIA

Pneumonia presents with a wide range of clinical and physiological signs that healthcare providers must recognize promptly to ensure timely and effective treatment. This lesson delves into these signs, emphasizing the importance of thorough clinical assessment and understanding the underlying physiological changes

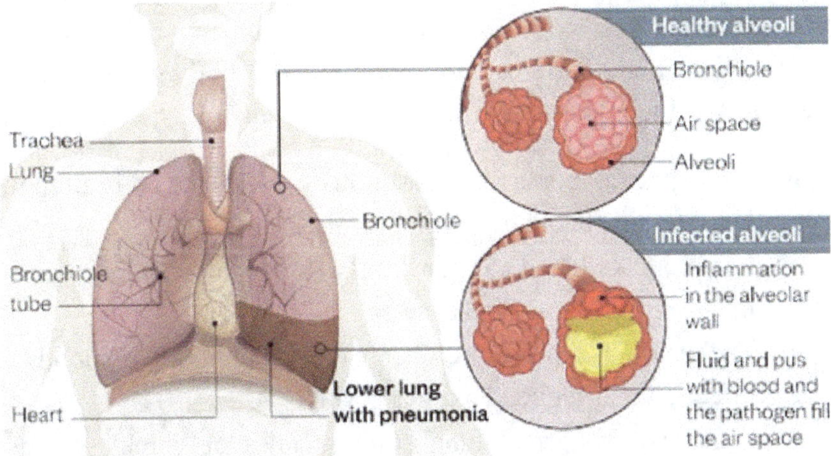

Clinical Presentation

The clinical presentation of pneumonia can vary depending on the causative pathogen, the patient's age, and the presence of any underlying health conditions. However, some common signs and **symptoms are observed in most cases:**

- Cough: A persistent cough that may produce mucus (sputum), which can be green, yellow, or tinged with blood.
- Fever: High fever is common, often accompanied by sweating and chills.
- Shortness of Breath: Difficulty breathing or rapid, shallow breathing.

- Chest Pain: Sharp or stabbing chest pain that worsens with deep breathing or coughing.
- Fatigue: General malaise and fatigue.
- Loss of Appetite: Decreased appetite and low energy levels.
- Nausea and Vomiting: Particularly in children, nausea and vomiting may occur.
- Confusion: Older adults may experience confusion or changes in mental status.

Physiological Signs

Physiological signs of pneumonia reflect the body's response to infection and the impact on respiratory function:

- Tachypnea: An increased respiratory rate as the body attempts to maintain adequate oxygen levels.
- Hypoxia: Reduced oxygen levels in the blood, which can be measured using pulse oximetry.
- Tachycardia: An elevated heart rate as the body responds to infection and reduced oxygen levels.
- Crackles: Abnormal lung sounds (rales or crackles) heard during auscultation, caused by the movement of fluid within the alveoli.
- Dullness to Percussion: A dull sound when tapping on the chest wall, indicating fluid or consolidation in the lungs.
- Increased Work of Breathing: Use of accessory muscles to breathe, nasal flaring, and intercostal retractions.

Pathophysiological Mechanisms

- Understanding the pathophysiological mechanisms behind these signs is crucial for effective management. The inflammation and infection in the lungs lead to alveolar consolidation, where the alveoli fill with fluid, pus, and cellular debris. This impairs gas exchange, leading to hypoxia and increased work of breathing.

- The body's immune response to infection results in the release of cytokines and other inflammatory mediators, which contribute to fever, increased heart rate, and systemic symptoms. In severe cases, the infection can spread to the bloodstream, leading to sepsis, a life-threatening condition.

Differential Diagnosis

Several conditions can mimic the clinical presentation of pneumonia, making differential diagnosis important. These conditions include:

- Bronchitis: Inflammation of the bronchial tubes, often presenting with a persistent cough and mucus production but without significant lung consolidation.
- Chronic Obstructive Pulmonary Disease (COPD) Exacerbation: Worsening of COPD symptoms, which can include increased cough, sputum production, and dyspnea.
- Pulmonary Embolism: A blood clot in the lung, presenting with sudden onset of shortness of breath, chest pain, and hypoxia.
- Heart Failure: Fluid accumulation in the lungs due to heart failure can mimic pneumonia, presenting with shortness of breath and abnormal lung sounds.
- Lung Cancer: Can present with a persistent cough, hemoptysis, and weight loss, along with abnormal findings on chest imaging.

Diagnostic Approach

A systematic diagnostic approach is essential for accurately diagnosing pneumonia and distinguishing it from other conditions:

- Clinical Assessment: A thorough history and physical examination to identify key signs and symptoms.
- Imaging: Chest X-ray remains the primary imaging modality, with CT scans used in more complex cases.

- Laboratory Tests: Blood tests to assess for infection, inflammation, and organ function. Sputum culture and blood cultures to identify the causative pathogen.
- Pulse Oximetry: To measure oxygen saturation levels and assess the severity of hypoxia.
- Additional Tests: In certain cases, additional tests such as bronchoscopy or pleural fluid analysis may be necessary.
- Recognizing the clinical and physiological signs of pneumonia is critical for timely diagnosis and effective management. A thorough understanding of these signs, along with a systematic diagnostic approach, enables healthcare providers to distinguish pneumonia from other conditions and initiate appropriate treatment.

DISCUSSION QUESTIONS

- How can healthcare providers differentiate between pneumonia and other respiratory illnesses based on clinical signs and symptoms?
- What are the challenges in diagnosing pneumonia in elderly patients, and what strategies can be employed to improve accuracy?

MODULE TWO

LESSON ONE: RADIOLOGICAL DIAGNOSIS

Radiological imaging plays a crucial role in the diagnosis and management of pneumonia. Chest X-rays are the most common imaging modality used to identify pneumonia and assess its severity. This lesson provides an in-depth look at the radiological signs of pneumonia, how to interpret chest X-rays, and the role of advanced imaging techniques.

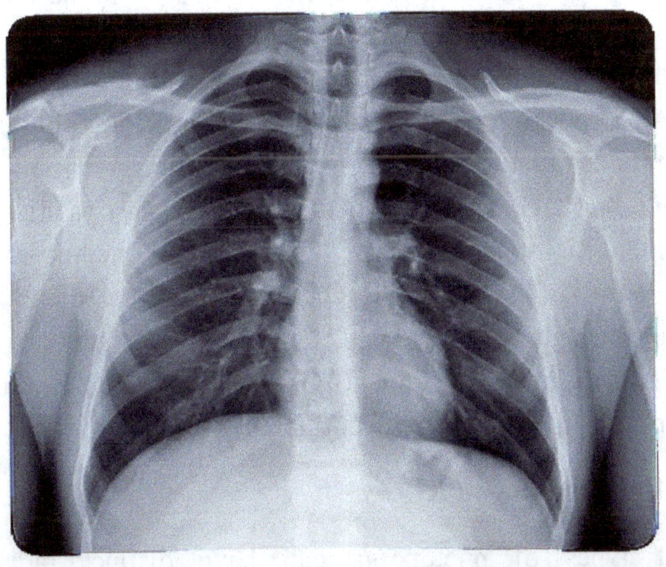

Basic Principles of Chest X-Ray Interpretation

Interpreting a chest X-ray involves a systematic approach to identify abnormalities and assess the overall lung and chest structure. Key principles include:

- Patient Positioning: Ensuring proper positioning (posteroanterior or anteroposterior views) to obtain accurate images.

- Image Quality: Assessing the quality of the X-ray, including exposure, rotation, and penetration.
- Systematic Review: Reviewing the image systematically, starting from the outside (soft tissues, bones) and moving inward (lungs, mediastinum).

Radiological Signs of Pneumonia

The radiological appearance of pneumonia can vary depending on the type and severity of the infection. Common radiological signs include:

- seen Consolidation: Homogeneous opacity in the lung fields due to alveolar filling with exudate, often as a white area on the X-ray.
- Air Bronchograms: Visible air-filled bronchi within the areas of consolidation, indicating alveolar filling.
- Interstitial Patterns: Reticular or nodular opacities in the interstitial spaces, seen in viral or atypical pneumonias.
- Pleural Effusion: Fluid accumulation in the pleural space, appearing as a blunted costophrenic angle or meniscus sign.
- Cavitation: Formation of cavities within the lung tissue, seen in necrotizing pneumonia or abscess formation.

Types of Pneumonia on X-Ray

Different types of pneumonia can have distinct radiological appearances:

- Lobar Pneumonia: Characterized by consolidation in one or more lobes of the lung, often caused by Streptococcus pneumoniae.
- Bronchopneumonia: Patchy areas of consolidation around the bronchi, commonly seen in bacterial pneumonia.
- Interstitial Pneumonia: Diffuse interstitial infiltrates, often associated with viral or atypical pneumonia.

- Aspiration Pneumonia: Consolidation in dependent lung segments, usually the lower lobes, due to aspiration of material.

Advanced Imaging Techniques

While chest X-rays are the primary imaging modality for pneumonia, advanced imaging techniques can provide additional information in complex cases:

- Computed Tomography (CT) Scan: Offers detailed cross-sectional images of the chest, useful for identifying complications, assessing the extent of disease, and detecting conditions that may mimic pneumonia.
- Ultrasound: Can be used to assess pleural effusions and guide thoracentesis.
- Magnetic Resonance Imaging (MRI): Rarely used but can provide detailed images of soft tissues and is useful in certain clinical scenarios.

Case Studies and Practical Applications

Understanding the radiological signs of pneumonia is enhanced by reviewing case studies and practical examples:

- Case Study 1: A 45-year-old male with high fever, productive cough, and left lower lobe consolidation on X-ray, diagnosed with bacterial lobar pneumonia.
- Case Study 2: A 60-year-old female with COPD and patchy infiltrates on X-ray, diagnosed with bronchopneumonia.
- Case Study 3: A 35-year-old male with diffuse interstitial infiltrates on X-ray, diagnosed with viral pneumonia.

Radiological imaging is a vital tool in the diagnosis and management of pneumonia. Understanding the key radiological signs, how to interpret chest X-rays systematically, and the role of advanced imaging techniques equips healthcare providers with the necessary skills to accurately diagnose and manage pneumonia.

DISCUSSION QUESTIONS

- How do the physiological changes associated with pneumonia impact the overall function of the respiratory system?
- What ways can understanding the pathophysiology of pneumonia help healthcare providers develop more effective treatment plans?

LESSON TWO: TREATMENT STRATEGIES MEDICATIONS AND THERAPIES

Effective treatment of pneumonia involves a combination of antimicrobial therapy, supportive care, and addressing any underlying conditions. This lesson provides a detailed overview of the various treatment strategies, including the choice of antibiotics, antiviral and antifungal therapies, and supportive treatments.

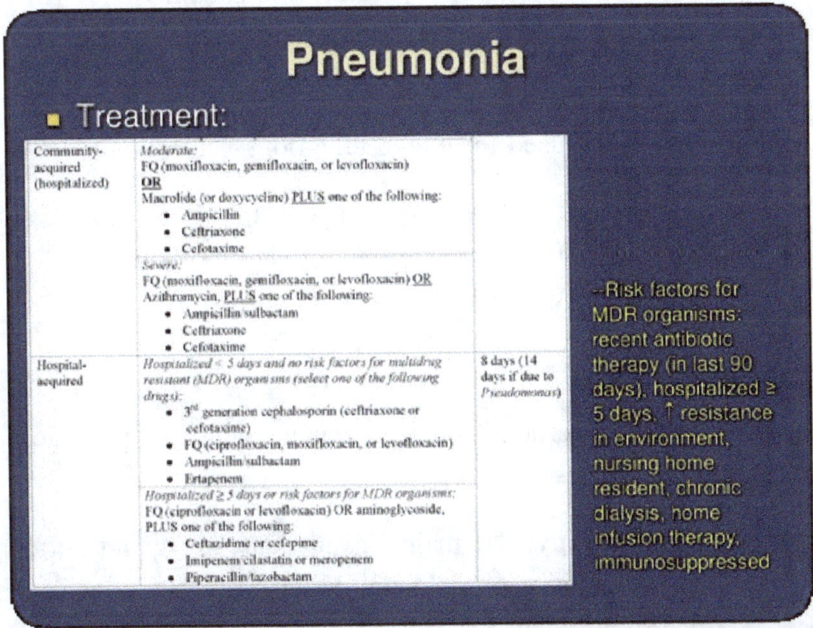

Pneumonia

Treatment:

Community-acquired (hospitalized)	*Moderate:* FQ (moxifloxacin, gemifloxacin, or levofloxacin) **OR** Macrolide (or doxycycline) <u>PLUS</u> one of the following: • Ampicillin • Ceftriaxone • Cefotaxime	
	Severe: FQ (moxifloxacin, gemifloxacin, or levofloxacin) <u>OR</u> Azithromycin, <u>PLUS</u> one of the following: • Ampicillin/sulbactam • Ceftriaxone • Cefotaxime	
Hospital-acquired	*Hospitalized < 5 days and no risk factors for multidrug resistant (MDR) organisms (select one of the following drugs):* • 3rd generation cephalosporin (ceftriaxone or cefotaxime) • FQ (ciprofloxacin, moxifloxacin, or levofloxacin) • Ampicillin/sulbactam • Ertapenem *Hospitalized ≥ 5 days or risk factors for MDR organisms:* FQ (ciprofloxacin or levofloxacin) OR aminoglycoside, PLUS one of the following: • Ceftazidime or cefepime • Imipenem/cilastatin or meropenem • Piperacillin/tazobactam	8 days (14 days if due to *Pseudomonas*)

Antimicrobial Therapy

The choice of antimicrobial therapy depends on the suspected or confirmed causative pathogen, the severity of the disease, and the patient's clinical condition.

1. Bacterial Pneumonia:

Antibiotics are the cornerstone of treatment. Commonly used antibiotics include:

- Beta-lactams: Such as penicillin and cephalosporins (e.g., amoxicillin, ceftriaxone).
- Macrolides: Such as azithromycin and clarithromycin.
- Fluoroquinolones: Such as levofloxacin and moxifloxacin.
- Tetracyclines: Such as doxycycline.

2. Viral Pneumonia:

Antiviral agents are used based on the specific virus involved:

- Influenza: Oseltamivir (Tamiflu) or zanamivir.
- RSV: Ribavirin in severe cases.

3. Fungal Pneumonia:

Antifungal agents are used for fungal infections:

- Histoplasmosis, Coccidioidomycosis: Itraconazole or fluconazole.
- Aspergillosis: Voriconazole or amphotericin B.

Supportive Care

Supportive care is crucial in the management of pneumonia, especially in severe cases:

- Oxygen Therapy: To maintain adequate oxygen saturation levels, delivered via nasal cannula, face mask, or mechanical ventilation in severe cases.
- Hydration: Maintaining fluid balance to prevent dehydration and support overall health.
- Antipyretics: Such as acetaminophen or ibuprofen to manage fever and reduce discomfort.
- Analgesics: For pain relief, especially if pleuritic chest pain is present.
- Respiratory Support: Including bronchodilators and chest physiotherapy to improve airway clearance and lung function.

Managing Complications

Complications of pneumonia can significantly impact patient outcomes and require prompt and effective management:

- Pleural Effusion: Drainage through thoracentesis or chest tube placement.
- Empyema: Management with antibiotics and drainage, sometimes requiring surgery.
- Sepsis: Aggressive management with intravenous fluids, antibiotics, and supportive care in an intensive care setting.
- Respiratory Failure: Mechanical ventilation and intensive respiratory support.

Special Considerations

Certain patient populations require special considerations in the treatment of pneumonia:

- Elderly Patients: May present atypically and have multiple comorbidities. Careful management of polypharmacy and monitoring for adverse effects of medications is essential.
- Children: Pediatric dosing of medications and consideration of different causative pathogens (e.g., RSV, Haemophilus influenzae type b).
- Immunocompromised Patients: Such as those with HIV/AIDS, cancer, or on immunosuppressive therapy. Broader spectrum antibiotics and antifungal agents may be required.

Emerging Therapies

Ongoing research continues to explore new treatment options for pneumonia:

- Monoclonal Antibodies: Targeting specific pathogens or inflammatory pathways.

- Antimicrobial Stewardship: Programs to optimize the use of antibiotics and reduce resistance.
- Vaccines: Development of new vaccines for prevention of pneumonia caused by different pathogens.

The effective treatment of pneumonia involves a combination of antimicrobial therapy, supportive care, and managing complications. Understanding the principles of treatment, the choice of appropriate medications, and the importance of supportive care equips healthcare providers to deliver optimal patient outcomes. This lesson provides a comprehensive guide to treatment strategies, preparing readers for discussions on managing complications and patient care in the following lesson.

DISCUSSION QUESTIONS

- What are the advantages and limitations of using chest X-rays versus CT scans in diagnosing pneumonia?
- How can advancements in imaging technology improve the early detection and management of pneumonia?

MODULE THREE

LESSON ONE: MANAGING COMPLICATIONS AND CO-MORBIDITIES

Pneumonia can lead to various complications and often occurs in patients with underlying co-morbidities. This lesson focuses on identifying and managing these complications and integrating care for co-morbid conditions to improve patient outcomes.

Common Complications of Pneumonia

1. **Pleural Effusion:** The accumulation of fluid in the pleural space, which can cause significant respiratory distress.
   - Diagnosis: Confirmed by chest X-ray or ultrasound.
   - Management: Thoracentesis for diagnostic and therapeutic purposes; chest tube placement in severe cases.
2. **Empyema**: Collection of pus in the pleural space, often following pleural effusion.

- Diagnosis: Confirmed by imaging and pleural fluid analysis.
- Management: Antibiotics and drainage, sometimes requiring surgical intervention.

3. **Lung Abscess**: Localized collection of pus within the lung tissue, resulting from necrotizing pneumonia.
   - Diagnosis: Confirmed by chest X-ray or CT scan.
   - Management: Prolonged antibiotic therapy and drainage if necessary.

4. **Sepsis**: A severe systemic response to infection, leading to organ dysfunction.
   - Diagnosis: Based on clinical criteria and laboratory tests (e.g., blood cultures, lactate levels).
   - Management: Aggressive fluid resuscitation, broad-spectrum antibiotics, and supportive care in an ICU setting.

5. **Acute Respiratory Distress Syndrome (ARDS)**: Severe inflammation and fluid accumulation in the alveoli, leading to respiratory failure.
   - Diagnosis: Based on clinical presentation and imaging findings.
   - Management: Mechanical ventilation and supportive care.

Managing Co-morbidities

Patients with co-morbid conditions require an integrated approach to manage pneumonia effectively:

1. **Chronic Obstructive Pulmonary Disease (COPD)**: Patients with COPD are at higher risk of pneumonia and may have exacerbations.
   - Management: Optimize COPD treatment, use of bronchodilators, and corticosteroids as needed.

2. **Heart Disease**: Pneumonia can exacerbate heart failure and other cardiac conditions.
   - Management: Careful fluid management and monitoring of cardiac function.

3. **Diabetes**: Diabetic patients are more susceptible to infections and complications.
    - Management: Strict glycemic control and monitoring for signs of complications
4. **Chronic Kidney Disease**: Patients may have altered pharmacokinetics for certain medications.
    - Management: Adjust dosing of antibiotics and other medications, monitor renal function.
5. **Immunosuppressed Patients**: Such as those with HIV/AIDS, cancer, or on immunosuppressive therapy.
    - Management: Broad-spectrum antibiotics, prophylactic antifungal or antiviral agents, and close monitoring for complications.

Integrating Care

Integrating care for patients with pneumonia and co-morbidities involves a multidisciplinary approach:

1. Collaboration: Between primary care providers, specialists (e.g., pulmonologists, cardiologists), and other healthcare professionals (e.g., respiratory therapists, pharmacists).
2. Care Coordination: Ensuring continuity of care and follow-up to monitor for complications and recurrence.
3. Patient Education: Educating patients about managing their underlying conditions and recognizing early signs of pneumonia.

Case Studies

Reviewing case studies can provide practical insights into managing complications and co-morbidities:

1. **Case Study 1:** A 70-year-old male with COPD and pneumonia, presenting with pleural effusion and requiring thoracentesis and antibiotics.

2. **Case Study 2:** A 65-year-old female with heart failure and pneumonia, requiring careful fluid management and cardiac monitoring.
3. **Case Study 3**: A 50-year-old male with diabetes and lung abscess, managed with prolonged antibiotics and drainage.

Managing complications and co-morbidities in patients with pneumonia requires a comprehensive and integrated approach. Recognizing common complications, understanding the interplay between pneumonia and co-morbid conditions, and implementing effective management strategies are essential for improving patient outcomes. This lesson equips healthcare providers with the knowledge and skills to address these challenges, preparing them for discussions on patient care and preventive measures in the following lesson.

DISCUSSION QUESTIONS

- How do treatment protocols differ between community-acquired pneumonia and hospital-acquired pneumonia?
- What are the potential side effects of common pneumonia medications, and how can healthcare providers manage them?

LESSON TWO: PATIENT CARE AND SUPPORT: BEST PRACTICES

Optimal patient care and support are essential components of pneumonia management. This lesson explores best practices for patient care, emphasizing the importance of a holistic and patient-centered approach to improve outcomes and enhance the quality of life for patients with pneumonia.

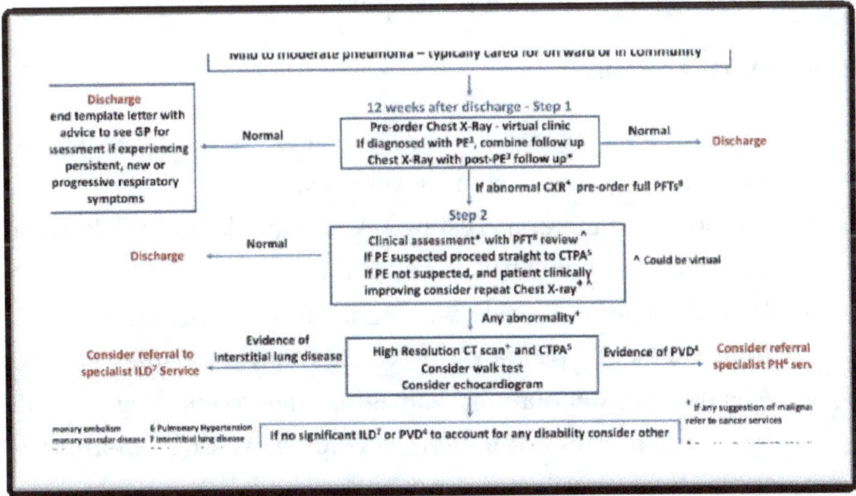

Nursing Care

Nursing care plays a crucial role in the management of pneumonia, providing essential support and interventions:

- Assessment and Monitoring: Regular monitoring of vital signs, oxygen saturation, and respiratory status. Early recognition of changes in condition and prompt intervention.
- Oxygen Therapy: Administering and titrating oxygen therapy to maintain adequate oxygen levels. Monitoring for signs of hypoxia and adjusting therapy as needed.

- Medication Administration: Ensuring timely and accurate administration of prescribed medications, including antibiotics, antivirals, and supportive medications.
- Hydration and Nutrition: Maintaining adequate hydration and nutritional support, considering the patient's needs and preferences. Monitoring for signs of dehydration or malnutrition.
- Airway Clearance: Encouraging effective coughing and deep breathing exercises. Providing chest physiotherapy and suctioning as needed to maintain airway patency.

Respiratory Therapy

- Respiratory therapists play a vital role in managing pneumonia, particularly in severe cases:
- Pulmonary Function Testing: Assessing lung function and identifying any underlying respiratory issues.
- Bronchodilator Therapy: Administering bronchodilators to improve airway patency and reduce bronchospasm.
- Mechanical Ventilation: Managing and monitoring patients on mechanical ventilation, including setting appropriate ventilator parameters and weaning protocols.
- Non-Invasive Ventilation: Using techniques such as CPAP or BiPAP to support patients with respiratory distress.

Patient Education

Educating patients about pneumonia, its management, and preventive measures is crucial for promoting recovery and preventing recurrence:

- Disease Understanding: Providing clear and concise information about pneumonia, its causes, symptoms, and treatment.

- Medication Adherence: Educating patients on the importance of completing the full course of prescribed medications, even if symptoms improve.
- Symptom Management: Teaching patients how to manage symptoms at home, including cough, fever, and shortness of breath.
- Follow-Up Care: Emphasizing the importance of follow-up appointments and monitoring for any signs of complications or recurrence.

Psychosocial Support

Addressing the psychosocial aspects of pneumonia is important for overall patient well-being:

- Emotional Support: Providing emotional support and counseling to patients and their families, addressing any fears or concerns.
- Social Support: Connecting patients with support groups, community resources, and social services to assist with practical needs.
- Mental Health: Assessing for signs of depression or anxiety and referring patients to mental health services if needed.

Best Practices in Care Coordination

Effective care coordination involves a multidisciplinary approach, ensuring seamless communication and collaboration among healthcare providers:

- Care Plans: Developing individualized care plans that address the specific needs and preferences of each patient.
- Communication: Facilitating open and effective communication among healthcare providers, patients, and families.

- Transitions of Care: Ensuring smooth transitions between different levels of care, such as from hospital to home or to a rehabilitation facility.

Case Studies and Practical Applications

Reviewing case studies can provide valuable insights into best practices for patient care and support:

- Case Study 1: A 75-year-old female with pneumonia and multiple co-morbidities, managed with a multidisciplinary approach and comprehensive care plan.
- Case Study 2: A 40-year-old male with severe pneumonia requiring mechanical ventilation, highlighting the role of respiratory therapy and care coordination.
- Case Study 3: A 60-year-old male with recurrent pneumonia, emphasizing the importance of patient education and follow-up care.

Providing optimal patient care and support is essential for managing pneumonia effectively and improving patient outcomes. This lesson highlights best practices in nursing care, respiratory therapy, patient education, psychosocial support, and care coordination. By adopting a holistic and patient-centered approach, healthcare providers can enhance the quality of life for patients with pneumonia and support their recovery journey.

DISCUSSION QUESTIONS

- How do the clinical manifestations of pneumonia vary between different age groups and comorbid conditions?
- How do the clinical manifestations of pneumonia vary between different age groups and comorbid conditions?

MODULE FOUR

LESSON ONE: PREVENTIVE MEASURES AND VACCINATION

Preventive measures and vaccination play a crucial role in reducing the incidence and severity of pneumonia. This lesson explores various strategies for preventing pneumonia, including vaccination, public health interventions, and patient education.

Vaccination

Vaccination is one of the most effective ways to prevent pneumonia caused by certain pathogens. Key vaccines include:

1. **Pneumococcal Vaccines**: Protect against Streptococcus pneumoniae.
   - PCV13 (Prevnar 13): Recommended for infants, young children, and adults with certain risk factors.

- PPSV23 (Pneumovax 23): Recommended for adults over 65 years and individuals with specific health conditions.

2. **Influenza Vaccine**: Protects against seasonal influenza, which can lead to viral pneumonia and secondary bacterial pneumonia.

   - Annual Vaccination: Recommended for all individuals over six months of age, with particular emphasis on high-risk groups.

3. **Other Vaccines**: Depending on the patient's risk factors and geographic location, additional vaccines may be recommended, such as:

   - Haemophilus influenzae type b (Hib) Vaccine: Especially for children.
   - Pertussis (Whooping Cough) Vaccine: Included in the DTaP and Tdap vaccines.
   - COVID-19 Vaccine: To prevent COVID-19, which can cause severe pneumonia.

Public Health Interventions

Public health interventions are essential for preventing pneumonia at the community level:

- Smoking Cessation: Smoking is a significant risk factor for pneumonia. Public health campaigns and smoking cessation programs can help reduce the incidence of pneumonia.
- Hand Hygiene: Promoting regular handwashing with soap and water to reduce the spread of respiratory infections.
- Respiratory Hygiene: Encouraging covering the mouth and nose when coughing or sneezing and using tissues or elbow to reduce transmission of pathogens.
- Environmental Controls: Improving air quality, reducing indoor pollution, and ensuring proper ventilation to decrease the risk of respiratory infections.

Patient Education

Educating patients about preventive measures is crucial for reducing the risk of pneumonia:

- Vaccination Awareness: Informing patients about the importance of vaccination and ensuring they receive recommended vaccines.
- Healthy Lifestyle: Encouraging a healthy lifestyle, including a balanced diet, regular exercise, adequate sleep, and smoking cessation.
- Recognizing Early Signs: Teaching patients to recognize the early signs of pneumonia and seek medical attention promptly.
- Adherence to Treatment: Emphasizing the importance of adhering to prescribed treatments and follow-up care.

Special Populations

Certain populations are at higher risk for pneumonia and require targeted preventive measures:

- Elderly: Higher susceptibility due to age-related changes in the immune system. Ensuring vaccination and promoting healthy aging practices.
- Children: High risk of respiratory infections. Ensuring vaccination and promoting good hygiene practices.
- Immunocompromised Individuals: Increased risk due to weakened immune systems. Tailored vaccination schedules and preventive measures.

Global Initiatives

Global initiatives aim to reduce the burden of pneumonia worldwide:

- Global Action Plan for Pneumonia and Diarrhoea (GAPPD): Aims to reduce deaths from pneumonia and diarrhoea by promoting vaccination, appropriate case management, and improved nutrition.

- Gavi, the Vaccine Alliance: Supports vaccination programs in low-income countries to protect against pneumococcal disease and other infections.

Case Studies and Practical Applications

Case studies provide practical insights into preventive measures:

- Case Study 1: A 65-year-old male with chronic lung disease, highlighting the importance of pneumococcal and influenza vaccination.
- Case Study 2: A 2-year-old child with a history of recurrent respiratory infections, emphasizing the role of Hib and PCV13 vaccination.
- Case Study 3: A 45-year-old female smoker, illustrating the impact of smoking cessation programs and respiratory hygiene practices.

Preventive measures and vaccination are key strategies in reducing the incidence and severity of pneumonia. This lesson highlights the importance of vaccination, public health interventions, patient education, and targeted strategies for special populations. By implementing these preventive measures, healthcare providers can significantly reduce the burden of pneumonia and improve public health outcomes.

DISCUSSION QUESTIONS

- How does pneumonia presentation differ in immunocompromised patients compared to the general population?
- What are the specific challenges in managing pneumonia in pediatric patients, and what best practices can be employed?

LESSON TWO: FUTURE DIRECTIONS AND ADVANCEMENTS IN PNEUMONIA MANAGEMENT

The field of pneumonia management is continually evolving with advancements in research, technology, and clinical practices. This lesson explores future directions and potential breakthroughs in the prevention, diagnosis, and treatment of pneumonia.

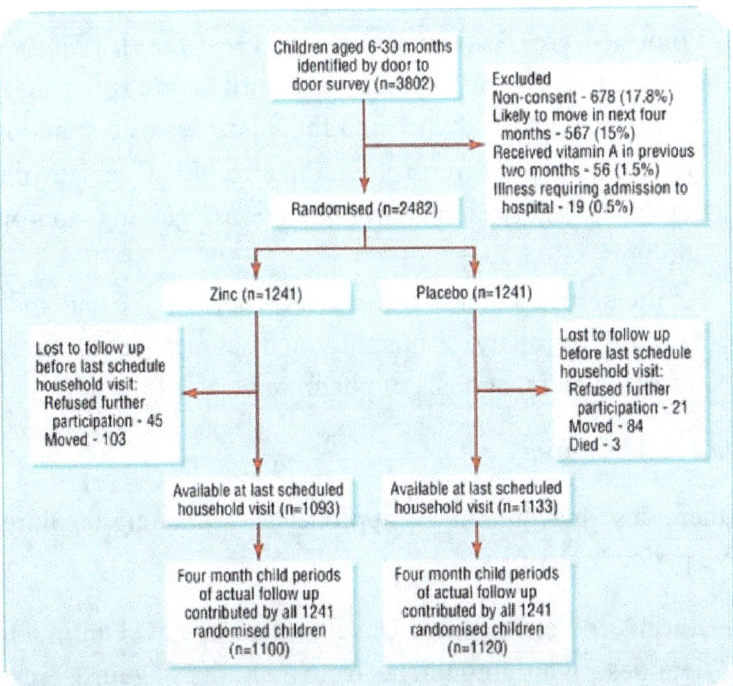

Advances in Vaccination

Ongoing research aims to develop more effective vaccines and expand coverage:

- Universal Pneumococcal Vaccine: Research is focused on developing a universal vaccine that provides broader protection against multiple strains of Streptococcus pneumoniae.

- Improved Influenza Vaccines: Efforts are underway to develop longer-lasting and more effective influenza vaccines, including universal influenza vaccines that provide broader protection.
- COVID-19 Vaccines: Continued development of vaccines to address emerging variants and improve efficacy and durability.

Novel Diagnostic Tools

Advancements in diagnostic tools can enhance the accuracy and speed of pneumonia diagnosis:

- Point-of-Care Testing: Development of rapid, point-of-care tests for early and accurate identification of pathogens, including bacterial, viral, and fungal causes of pneumonia.
- Biomarkers: Research into biomarkers that can distinguish between bacterial and viral infections, guiding appropriate antibiotic use.
- Artificial Intelligence (AI): Utilization of AI and machine learning to analyze imaging and clinical data for early detection and diagnosis of pneumonia.

Innovative Therapies

New therapies and treatment approaches are being explored to improve patient outcomes:

- Antimicrobial Peptides: Development of novel antimicrobial peptides with broad-spectrum activity against resistant pathogens.
- Phage Therapy: Use of bacteriophages to target and kill antibiotic-resistant bacteria.
- Immunomodulatory Therapies: Research into therapies that modulate the immune response to enhance the body's ability to fight infection.

Personalized Medicine

Personalized medicine approaches aim to tailor treatment to individual patient characteristics:

- Genomic Profiling: Utilizing genomic profiling to identify genetic factors that influence susceptibility to pneumonia and response to treatment.
- Precision Antibiotics: Development of precision antibiotics that target specific pathogens based on genetic and molecular profiles.
- Patient-Specific Treatment Plans: Creating individualized treatment plans based on patient's genetic makeup, co-morbidities, and other factors.

Telemedicine and Remote Monitoring

Telemedicine and remote monitoring technologies can enhance patient care and management:

- Teleconsultations: Providing remote consultations and follow-up care, especially for patients in rural or underserved areas.
- Remote Monitoring: Using wearable devices and remote monitoring systems to track patient's vital signs and respiratory status, enabling early intervention.

Global Health Initiatives

Global health initiatives continue to play a crucial role in combating pneumonia:

- Strengthening Health Systems: Efforts to strengthen health systems in low- and middle-income countries, improving access to vaccines, diagnostics, and treatment.

- Research Collaboration: Promoting international collaboration and research to address global challenges in pneumonia management.
- Education and Training: Enhancing education and training for healthcare providers on best practices in pneumonia prevention and management.

Case Studies and Future Scenarios

Exploring future scenarios and case studies provides insights into the potential impact of advancements:

- Case Study 1: A 70-year-old male with a history of COPD and recurrent pneumonia, managed with personalized medicine approaches and remote monitoring.
- Case Study 2: A 50-year-old female with antibiotic-resistant pneumonia, treated with phage therapy and novel antimicrobial peptides.
- Case Study 3: A community health initiative in a low-income country, utilizing global health strategies and telemedicine to reduce the burden of pneumonia.

The future of pneumonia management holds promise with advancements in vaccination, diagnostic tools, innovative therapies, personalized medicine, telemedicine, and global health initiatives. This lesson highlights the potential breakthroughs and future directions that can transform pneumonia prevention, diagnosis, and treatment. By embracing these advancements, healthcare providers can improve patient outcomes, reduce the burden of pneumonia, and enhance public health worldwide.

DISCUSSION QUESTIONS

- What role do vaccines play in the prevention of pneumonia, and how can healthcare providers increase vaccination rates?

- How can public health initiatives and education campaigns effectively reduce the incidence of pneumonia in high-risk populations?

MODULE FIVE

LESSON ONE: ADDRESSING ANTIBIOTIC RESISTANCE IN PNEUMONIA TREATMENT

Antibiotic resistance is a significant challenge in the treatment of pneumonia. This lesson delves into the causes, implications, and strategies for addressing antibiotic resistance, emphasizing the importance of antimicrobial stewardship.

Gram Positive Antibiotics w/ MRSA Activity	Gram Negative Antibiotics with Anti-Pseudomonal Activity: B-Lactam Agents	Gram Negative Antibiotics with Anti-Pseudomonal Activity: Non-B-Lactam-Based Agents
Glycopeptides Vancomycin 15mg/kg IV q8 – 12h (Consider Loading Dose of 25-30mg/kg x1 for Severe Illness) OR Oxazolidinones Linezolid 600mg IV q12h	Antipseudomonal Penicillins Piperacillin-Tazobactam 4.5g IV q6h OR Cephalosporins Cefepime 2g IV q8h Ceftazidime 2g IV q8h OR Carbepenems Imipenem 500mg IV q6h Meropenem 1g IV q8h OR Monobactams Aztreonam 2g IVq8h	Fluoroquinolones Ciprofloxacin 400mg IV q8h Levofloxacin 750mg IV q24h OR Aminoglycosides Amikacin 15 – 20mg/kg IV q24h Gentamicin 5 – 7 mg/kg IV q24h Tobramycin 5 – 7mg/kg IV q24h OR Polymyxins Colistin 5mg/kg IV x1 (Loading Dose) followed by 2.5mg x (1.5 x CrCl + 30) IV q12h (Maintenance Dose) Polymyxin B 2.5 – 3.0 mg/kg/d Divided in 2 Daily IV Doses

Understanding Antibiotic Resistance

Antibiotic resistance occurs when bacteria evolve mechanisms to withstand the effects of antibiotics designed to kill them. Key factors contributing to antibiotic resistance include:

- Overuse of Antibiotics: Frequent and inappropriate use of antibiotics in healthcare settings and agriculture.
- Incomplete Courses: Patients not completing prescribed antibiotic courses, allowing some bacteria to survive and develop resistance.

- Hospital Environments: Hospitals can be breeding grounds for resistant bacteria due to the high use of antibiotics and close quarters of sick patients.

Impact on Pneumonia Treatment

Antibiotic resistance complicates the treatment of pneumonia by:

- Reducing Efficacy: Common antibiotics may become less effective or ineffective, requiring alternative treatments.
- Increasing Morbidity and Mortality: Resistant infections are harder to treat, leading to longer hospital stays, increased medical costs, and higher mortality rates.
- Limited Options: Fewer treatment options may be available for resistant infections, necessitating the use of more toxic or less effective drugs.

Strategies for Combating Antibiotic Resistance

Addressing antibiotic resistance requires a multifaceted approach:

- Antimicrobial Stewardship Programs: Implementing programs to optimize antibiotic use, ensuring the right antibiotic, dose, and duration.
- Education and Awareness: Educating healthcare providers and the public about the dangers of antibiotic resistance and the importance of appropriate use.
- Surveillance and Reporting: Monitoring antibiotic resistance patterns and reporting data to inform treatment guidelines and policies.
- Research and Development: Investing in research to develop new antibiotics and alternative therapies, such as phage therapy and antimicrobial peptides.

Clinical Guidelines and Protocols

Developing and adhering to clinical guidelines is crucial for managing antibiotic resistance:

- Empirical Therapy: Using evidence-based guidelines to choose initial antibiotic therapy based on local resistance patterns and patient factors.
- De-escalation: Adjusting antibiotic therapy based on culture results and clinical response to minimize the use of broad-spectrum antibiotics.
- Infection Control: Implementing strict infection control measures in healthcare settings to prevent the spread of resistant bacteria.

Role of Healthcare Providers

Healthcare providers play a key role in combating antibiotic resistance:

- Judicious Prescribing: Avoiding unnecessary antibiotic prescriptions and choosing appropriate agents.
- Patient Education: Informing patients about the importance of taking antibiotics as prescribed and the risks of resistance.
- Advocacy: Advocating for policies that promote antimicrobial stewardship and support research efforts.

Case Studies and Best Practices

Reviewing case studies can provide practical insights into addressing antibiotic resistance:

- Case Study 1: A hospital implementing an antimicrobial stewardship program, resulting in reduced antibiotic use and lower resistance rates.

- Case Study 2: A patient with multidrug-resistant pneumonia successfully treated with a combination of newer antibiotics and supportive care.
- Case Study 3: A community education campaign reducing antibiotic misuse and resistance in a rural population.

Addressing antibiotic resistance in pneumonia treatment is critical for ensuring effective patient care and improving outcomes. This lesson highlights the causes and impacts of resistance, strategies for combating it, and the essential role of healthcare providers in this effort. By implementing these strategies, the healthcare community can mitigate the challenges of antibiotic resistance and enhance the management of pneumonia.

DISCUSSION QUESTIONS

- What strategies can healthcare providers implement to reduce the overuse of antibiotics and combat antibiotic resistance?
- How can antimicrobial stewardship programs be effectively integrated into clinical practice to manage pneumonia treatment?

MODULE SIX

LESSON ONE: INTEGRATING TECHNOLOGY IN PNEUMONIA MANAGEMENT

Advancements in technology are transforming the management of pneumonia, offering new tools and approaches to improve diagnosis, treatment, and patient care. This lesson explores the integration of technology in pneumonia management, from telemedicine to artificial intelligence.

Telemedicine and Remote Monitoring

Telemedicine provides opportunities for remote diagnosis, treatment, and follow-up care:

- Virtual Consultations: Enabling patients to receive medical advice and treatment plans through video calls, reducing the need for in-person visits.

- Remote Monitoring Devices: Utilizing wearable devices to monitor vital signs and respiratory status, allowing for early intervention and continuous care.
- Telehealth Platforms: Offering comprehensive telehealth services, including medication management and patient education.

Artificial Intelligence (AI) and Machine Learning

AI and machine learning are revolutionizing pneumonia diagnosis and treatment:

- AI-Driven Diagnostics: Using AI algorithms to analyze imaging data, such as chest X-rays and CT scans, for early and accurate pneumonia detection.
- Predictive Analytics: Employing machine learning to predict disease progression and outcomes, aiding in personalized treatment planning.
- Clinical Decision Support Systems: Integrating AI into electronic health records (EHRs) to provide real-time decision support for clinicians.

Advanced Imaging Techniques

Innovations in imaging technology enhance the diagnosis and monitoring of pneumonia:

- High-Resolution CT Scans: Providing detailed images of the lungs to identify pneumonia and assess severity.
- Ultrasound: Offering a non-invasive and portable option for diagnosing pleural effusions and guiding procedures like thoracentesis.
- MRI: Occasionally used to evaluate complex cases where other imaging modalities are inconclusive.

Mobile Health Applications

Mobile health (mHealth) apps offer new ways to engage patients and support pneumonia management:

- Symptom Trackers: Allowing patients to log symptoms and receive personalized advice based on their inputs.
- Medication Reminders: Helping patients adhere to their prescribed treatment regimens through reminders and alerts.
- Educational Resources: Providing access to information on pneumonia prevention, treatment, and self-care.

Genomic and Molecular Technologies

Genomic and molecular technologies contribute to personalized pneumonia care:

- Genetic Testing: Identifying genetic predispositions to severe pneumonia and guiding targeted therapies.
- Molecular Diagnostics: Using PCR and other molecular techniques to rapidly identify causative pathogens and tailor antibiotic therapy.
- Biomarker Discovery: Researching biomarkers for early detection and monitoring of pneumonia progression and response to treatment.

Case Studies and Future Applications

Exploring case studies and future applications illustrates the potential of technology in pneumonia management:

- Case Study 1: A hospital implementing AI-driven diagnostic tools, leading to faster and more accurate pneumonia diagnoses.
- Case Study 2: A telemedicine program providing remote care for pneumonia patients in a rural community, improving access and outcomes.

- Case Study 3: A mobile health app aiding in patient adherence to treatment and follow-up care, reducing readmission rates.

Integrating technology into pneumonia management offers significant opportunities to enhance diagnosis, treatment, and patient care. This lesson highlights the role of telemedicine, AI, advanced imaging, mHealth applications, and genomic technologies in revolutionizing pneumonia care. By embracing these technological advancements, healthcare providers can improve outcomes and transform the management of pneumonia, paving the way for a more connected and efficient healthcare system.

DISCUSSION QUESTIONS

- How can telemedicine and remote monitoring improve the management of pneumonia in rural and underserved areas?
- What are the potential benefits and challenges of using artificial intelligence and machine learning in pneumonia diagnosis and treatment?

MODULE SEVEN

LESSON ONE: THE ROLE OF NUTRITION IN PNEUMONIA PREVENTION AND RECOVERY

Nutrition plays a vital role in the prevention and recovery of pneumonia. This lesson explores the impact of diet on immune function, specific nutrients that support respiratory health, and nutritional strategies for patients with pneumonia.

The Link Between Nutrition and Immune Function

A well-balanced diet enhances the immune system, making the body more resilient against infections like pneumonia. Key aspects include:

- Macronutrients: Adequate intake of carbohydrates, proteins, and fats to support overall health and energy levels.

- Micronutrients: Essential vitamins and minerals that play a critical role in immune function, such as vitamin C, vitamin D, zinc, and selenium.
- Hydration: Maintaining proper hydration to support bodily functions and mucosal defenses.

Key Nutrients for Respiratory Health

Certain nutrients have been shown to specifically support respiratory health and reduce the risk of pneumonia:

- Vitamin C: An antioxidant that boosts the immune system and supports lung function.
- Vitamin D: Regulates immune responses and has been linked to reduced respiratory infections.
- Zinc: Supports immune function and has antiviral properties.
- Omega-3 Fatty Acids: Found in fish oil, these reduce inflammation and support overall lung health.
- Probiotics: Beneficial bacteria that support gut health and immune function.

Dietary Recommendations for Prevention

To reduce the risk of pneumonia, individuals should follow a diet rich in:

- Fruits and Vegetables: High in vitamins, minerals, and antioxidants.
- Whole Grains: Provide sustained energy and essential nutrients.
- Lean Proteins: Important for immune function and muscle maintenance.
- Healthy Fats: Found in nuts, seeds, avocados, and fish, these support overall health.

Nutritional Strategies for Pneumonia Recovery

For patients recovering from pneumonia, specific nutritional strategies can aid in recovery:

- Caloric Intake: Ensuring sufficient caloric intake to meet increased energy needs during recovery.
- Protein: Increasing protein intake to support tissue repair and immune function.
- Hydration: Maintaining adequate fluid intake to prevent dehydration and support recovery.
- Small, Frequent Meals: Eating small, frequent meals to improve appetite and nutrient intake.
- Supplements: Considering vitamin and mineral supplements if dietary intake is insufficient.

Role of Nutritionists and Dietitians

Nutritionists and dietitians play a crucial role in supporting pneumonia patients:

- Personalized Nutrition Plans: Developing individualized nutrition plans based on patients' needs, preferences, and medical conditions.
- Nutritional Counseling: Providing education and support to help patients make healthy dietary choices.
- Monitoring and Adjusting: Regularly monitoring patients' nutritional status and adjusting plans as needed.

Case Studies and Practical Applications

Reviewing case studies can provide practical insights into the role of nutrition in pneumonia prevention and recovery:

- Case Study 1: A 60-year-old male with a history of respiratory infections, successfully reducing his pneumonia risk through dietary changes and supplementation.

- Case Study 2: A 75-year-old female recovering from severe pneumonia, benefiting from a personalized nutrition plan that improved her strength and immune function.
- Case Study 3: A community health program promoting nutritional education and access to healthy foods, resulting in reduced pneumonia incidence.

Nutrition is a key component of pneumonia prevention and recovery. This lesson highlights the importance of a balanced diet, essential nutrients, and personalized nutritional strategies for supporting respiratory health and immune function. By integrating nutritional approaches into pneumonia care, healthcare providers can enhance patient outcomes and promote overall health.

DISCUSSION QUESTIONS

- How can healthcare providers ensure that patients with pneumonia receive adequate nutrition to support their recovery?
- What specific dietary changes can be recommended to patients to reduce their risk of developing pneumonia?

<u>CONCLUSION</u>

Pneumonia remains a significant global health challenge, affecting millions of individuals each year. As healthcare providers, it is our duty to be well-versed in all aspects of pneumonia care, from understanding its pathophysiology and clinical manifestations to utilizing advanced diagnostic tools and providing effective treatments. This comprehensive eBook has aimed to equip respiratory therapists, doctors, and nurses with the knowledge and skills necessary to manage pneumonia with the highest standard of care. of care. Pneumonia remains a significant global health challenge, affecting millions of individuals each year. As healthcare providers, it is our duty to be well-versed in all aspects of pneumonia care, from understanding its pathophysiology and clinical manifestations to utilizing advanced diagnostic tools and providing effective treatments. This comprehensive eBook has aimed to equip respiratory therapists, doctors, and nurses with the knowledge and skills necessary to manage pneumonia with the highest standard of care.

REFERENCES

Brown, J. S., & Griffiths, M. (2020). *"Pneumonia in the Elderly: Diagnosis and Management"*. Journal of Geriatric Medicine,

Campbell, H., & Nair, H. (2017). *"Global Epidemiology of Pneumonia: Mortality and Morbidity"*

Dellinger, R. P., & Levy, M. M. (2018). *"Severe Pneumonia and Sepsis: Pathophysiology and Clinical Management"*.

File, T. M., & Marrie, T. J. (2019). "Burden of Community-Acquired Pneumonia in North American Adults". Clinical Infectious Diseases,

Johnson, R. F., & Baliga, M. (2021). "Antibiotic Resistance in Respiratory Infections: Current Challenges and Future Directions". Journal of Antimicrobial Chemotherapy,

Li, Y., & Zhang, H. (2016). "Role of Chest Imaging in the Diagnosis and Management of Pneumonia". Radiology Journal,

Madhi, S. A., & Klugman, K. P. (2016). "Vaccine Strategies to Prevent Pneumonia in Children and Adults". Vaccine,

Martinez, J. A., & Fernandez, A. (2017). "Pneumonia in Immunocompromised Patients: Challenges and Management Strategies". Clinical Pulmonary Medicine,

Murray, P. R., & Rosenthal, K. S. (2018). "Microbiological Aspects of Pneumonia: Pathogens and Pathogenesis". Medical Microbiology.

9 798330 263936